What's in My Heart

Jasmine Killings

BookLeaf
Publishing
India | USA | UK

Presentation by *BookLeaf Publishing*

Web: www.bookleafpub.com

E-mail: info@bookleafpub.com

ISBN: 978-93-5744-948-9

First edition 2022

DEDICATION

This Book Is Dedicated to Christopher And Stephanie Killings My Beloved Parents Whom Assignment on this earth Completed, December 08, 2015 / March 04,

As You Rest Eternally, I Proceed on, With your legacy, Teachings, Wisdom and knowledge instilled and Bestowed on me. Thank You! Lord For Allowing Those Two to be my Parents!

ACKNOWLEDGEMENT

I Would like to express my thanks and give all honor and glory to God! God And his abounding grace and mercy I am able to complete this assignment.

PREFACE

Completing my first assignment as a newly established Author, has been a Long Rocky, Riveting, Emotional road. As Well as Fun and Rewarding. All Praises Goes to God. Growing up I Was a a very shy, reserved, observant , modest young girl, I only communed with my parents, siblings, and close relatives. Being a Daughter of A Pastor, I Adapted a lot of Christian Morals, values, Respect-of God that have followed me through life. Unable to find my voice through speaking, I discovered it through writing. And through writing i am able to express myself in ways I never imagined. I Have a way of channeling what's in my heart out to the world! I believe that the content that is featured in my book, comes from my heart and not just mine but others , What others Can't express; or don't have the words to say, I'm Advocating on God's Behalf to deliver these words, bringing hope,encouragement, joy, along the way! [This book is not for everybody] And if you happen to come across it, Know that God loves you and something on the inside waiting for You Amen Be Blessed!

(Immerse In Moments of Prayer) "COVID 19

Let's Immerse in moments of prayer
And pray for victims battling COVID-19
　　We pray Healing
In Our Moments of Prayer
We reflect over those grieving loses
Related and Unrelated to Corona
　　God Fill their empty voids
Let's Immerse and pray for our frontline
Workers, Doctors, Nurses, truck driver
Law Enforcement
　　We say Thank you And May God Continue
To Strengthen you All
Let's Immerse in a Moment Of Prayer And Pray
For Our President
And Other Governing Officials
　　With our heads Bowed And our Hearts
Emphatic
Lord Hear Our Nation Pray!

To My Adversary

If You Going to play
I Will Pray
If You Attack
In Worship I Strike Back
Your Distract
Is Just a useless act
Stress
God About to bless
Your Mess
Is Evidence of my success
Don't waste your time
Because the divine will intervene
Defeated you remain

Word

Why Am I'm not Mad
Because I read the word
Slow to Anger, Great Understanding
Superb that word
Intense moments of stress
I be at my best
"Why"
Because I studied the word
Thy word hidden in my heart
Very Smart, That part
Peace ,love, joy success
Why
Because I meditated on the word
Focused and Undisturbed
Book of law I don't depart
Sounds Obsurb
This Word

Arise

I feel like it is something I need to do
Heavy unexplainable heavenly presence
wrapped around me
In my soul
I'm Burning and yearning
Arise, Becomes My Dominant thought
Arise, I made you strong i hear
Arise out of slothfulness
Arise from procrastination
Arise from depression
Life He gives
Abundantly he promises
Spiritual Death Take a Long vacation
Under Jesus Name
Dismantle every weapon
Meant to
Kill
Steal
Destroy
(Be Obliterated)
My Mouth utter words that my ear heareth
But my mind don't comprehend
My heart only understandeth
Arise And Be Great!

On the Floor

Today I pray in a different posture
""On the Floor"
In my room , I Lie on the floor with my arms
In a "o" position Hands connected
Head place on my o formation
Body laid flat, Eyes closed, Room Dark, Quiet
Head Cleared, mind blank
All Gratitude and thanksgiving fills my thoughts
On this Floor
I lay down, boldly at your throne "My"
Concerns,
Request
Burdens
On this Floor
I Deny Myself, Pick up my cross
And follow you
On this Floor
I surrender
All of Me
Unashamed
Unafraid
Less of me
More of you
Use me lord

As I get up
Amen

List

Here Is A list of things I Simply Will not do
without God
1. Nothing
Heres what I will do with God
1. Everything

Acceptance

Weep, weep until I'm fast asleep
The pain is too deep
It cuts through my soul, spirit, mind
Like two knives intertwined

Cry, I cry no relief
You are gone, I'm living in unbelief
To celebrate is right
But grieving is wrong

Lord fill my void
Heal me from the loss
As i lay loss
Life is different now

Help me to move on
As they moved on
To start eternity
As I grasp life eternally

Pray

When I wake
I'm Gone Pray
When I shower
I'm gone pray
When eat breakfast
I'm gone pray
Driving to work
I'm gone pray
On my lunch break
I'm gone pray
Kids acting up
I'm gone pay
Sad
Mad
Happy
Frustrated
I'm gone pray
Sick, well
I'm gone pray
Rich, Broke
I'm gone pray
Rain or shine,
I'm gone pray

Song

In My heart i have a song
Desiring a mic, I can sing
All night long
No Words exists

No Form, style or stanzas
Yet it full of verbs
Man ear never heard it
Yokes it will break,

In my head I hear it so beautifully
Melodies, Harmonies and rifts
Replaying over and over
I must set it free

Who is he

The man I love but can not see
Love unfailing I never known
Years of heartbreaks, failure, abuse
Was my daily use

But 'He' caught my heart
Right when my life was falling apart
Hearing about him I had to know more
I needed this mysterious deity attention
He love me, despite my life condition

Who is he I pondered
We began talking for hours
I would sing, play instruments in his honor
Being in alignment with book
Whew! Im hooked

My life is not the same
Since he came
Who is he you wonder
Open your hearts and you will see
His love is just not Just for me

Like Me

Sovereign God
I am broken
Like a limb off a tree
I heard the words spoken

Dirty like a dish rag
Stained, like spilled tea on white sheets
Lost like a airport bag
Can you love a sinner like me

I'm Ashamed to enter your presence
Shy like a kid on the first day of school
How can I present myself
Please lord, Hear My Plea!
Can you save a sinner like me!

Harvest

I Found the right location
Sunny with dappled shade
Fruits are at your discretion
Preparing the soil
Testing the Sand and Clay
Ph levels
I turned the soiled
Removed Rocks, roots
Planting dates have been observed
One by one I planted the seeds
Watering
I Watched over the plants as they grew
Fertilize, Fertilize
Lord I did what I could, to honor your word
Laboring in the fields days I grew weary
Faint not I did not
In due season I will reap the harvest
My Preparation been Good

P.R.A.Y

P_ ut your head down
R-Reflect, Reminisce
A-locate your thoughts
Y-Eli's to our fathers leading

Lift me up

Lift me up, lift me up
In your presence I stand yet again
The weight of the world is on my shoulder
I feel as if I'm carrying a Boulder
With a shaky voice I say

Lord lift me up, lift me up
I feel like I can't it anymore
Lift me up, lift me up
Weak I am, need you, I surely do

Hear, the thing in my chest beating
Boom, bah, boom, bah boom bah
It's calling out to you
Knees are bent, I keep repeating

Lord lift me up, lift me
Lift me, lift me, lift me
Bravely I speak,
I need you, I need you, I need you

Come pick me up, come lift me up lord

Embrace

Can I love you
As you love me
Experience your spirit
Warm embrace
Whilst your presence fills this place
I will sing new praises to you name

She

She
Who is she
I am she
You may who "She" Maybe
She- is Quiet: But her spirit is fierce
She_ is meek:her enemies are astray and at bay
She- is wise: prosperous, Empowered
She- is strong: draws strength from god
She- is mysterious: to know her spirit is to share
her spirit
She- is humble:: modest
She-is warrior: prayers moves mountains
She -is Dedicated- servant
She- is leader: Role Model, teacher, Advocate
She - is kind: loving and giving
She-is a mother: moral support , nurturing,
caring
Are you She just like me

Alone

Lord, you separated me from the rest
And deemed me blessed
I do stressed
But alone is best

All by myself
I conquer , rise, and strive
My focus stays on you
You always get me through

Alone with you I worship
In spirit and in truth
Our relationship is deeper than friendship
I'm in grandeur
When I'm alone with you

Spoken For

Sorry World I'm spoken For
He calls me by my name
He forgives me
He known me before I was born
Open arms he accepts me
Never lets me down
He keeps me everyone of his promises
He doesn't lie but keeps his word
In body he's absent , but his spirit comforts me
So Don't speak for me
I'm spoken for

Mistaken

You See, it's not pride!!
It's Content
I'm content in God
I'm content in the word
I'm content in prayer
I'm content in me!!!
It's not arrogance, Nor haughtiness, or conceited
It's just Jesu and I'm complete

www.ingramcontent.com/pod-product-compliance
Lightning Source LLC
LaVergne TN
LVHW050507210726

843509LV00015BA/3034